T. J. WESTIN

Man of the House

by Linda Sibley

Cover and Inside Illustrations: Dan Hatala

In memory of Michael Clayton Watson, who lost his battle with Lou Gehrig's disease on August 11, 1999

About the Author

Linda Sibley has lived in Harlingen, Texas, her entire life, except for one year away at school. She now lives there with her husband, Rick, and two children, Jeremy and Jennifer.

Ms. Sibley did contract work for attorneys for 15 years so she could be at home to raise her children. Now she is working at a local hospital part-time. This enables her to spend time writing, which is her favorite thing to do. She also enjoys reading and searching for interesting antiques.

Traveling is another of Ms. Sibley's interests. So far she has visited 24 states and 2 countries. She is always looking for an excuse to go on another trip.

PB ISBN-10: 0-7891-5610-3 ISBN-13: 978-0-7891-5610-5
RLB ISBN-10: 0-7569-0355-6 ISBN-13: 978-0-7569-0355-8
Printed in the U.S.A.

4 5 6 7 8 9 PP 13 12 11 10 09 08

Contents

A Brainstorm

"It's seven minutes until 4:00!" I shouted to Douglas. "Let's go!"

I didn't wait to see if he was following me. I just jumped on my old bike and took off. Once I was out of the school yard, I pedaled hard down the street. At the end of my driveway, I hit the brakes. My bike skidded all the way to the garage door.

It was probably one of my best skid marks yet. I'd have to remember to come back and measure it later.

I didn't take time to set the kickstand. I just let the bike fall on the soft grass. Douglas came skidding in behind me seconds later.

"Get the drinks!" I called to Douglas. "I'll put the popcorn in the microwave."

Douglas Logan and I are a team. We've been a team since our first day of school. I remember walking into the classroom with my stomach churning. When Mrs. Watson said hello, I almost threw up on her shoes. But then Douglas appeared.

I can still picture him standing in the doorway. He was smiling so big that his whole face was scrunched up. His curly black hair made his face look round. He was shorter than everyone else. He looks pretty much the same today—just a little older.

I don't look anything like I did back then. I've gone through a growth spurt that's left me tall and skinny. Most people say I look like my dad with my thick brown hair. I like to be compared to my dad. But it also makes me kind of sad.

My dad died when I was only seven years old. I was too young to understand about Lou Gehrig's disease then. I still don't totally understand it now. All I know for sure is that it took my dad away from me.

Douglas was always there for me during that time. Somehow he'd known when I needed a friend and when I just wanted to be alone. Six years have passed now, and he's still there for me. I suspect he always will be.

"Did you turn it to channel 22?" I asked Douglas.

Before he could answer, the announcer was saying, "Hello! Welcome to *Whiz Kid*—the game that can make a kid wealthy!"

Every day we were home by 4:00. We plopped down exactly three feet in front of the TV. Popcorn and sodas were our usual snack. We were sure that eating popcorn and drinking soda increased our brain power.

The contestants were always a boy and a girl. We usually cheered for the boys and booed the girls. Unless the girl was really cute.

Douglas and I usually played against each other. I always won. I don't know why. Answers sure didn't come that easy to me at school. But there was just something about the game. I seemed to know most of the answers without thinking about them.

"I know the first answer!" Douglas yelled. "It's Kansas City!"

"No!" I shot back. "The capital of Kansas is Topeka!"

"The answer is Topeka," said Russ Connor, the host of the show.

"How did you know that?" whined Douglas.

"I don't know," I said, shrugging my shoulders.

"Which fraction is the same as 3/4?" asked Russ. "Is it 5/8, 6/8, or 7/8?"

"It's 7/8!" Douglas shouted immediately.

"I think it's 6/8," I said confidently.

"The answer is 6/8," Russ confirmed.

The rest of the game went the same way. At the end, Douglas collapsed on the floor.

"I could never be on this show," he moaned.

As he said those words, something inside my brain clicked. I'd never even thought of being on the show myself. But the more I thought about it, the more I liked the idea. It would be a great way to make money. I could make more in one game than I could make all summer mowing yards.

"Maybe *I'll* try out for the show," I said thoughtfully.

Douglas sat up straight and stared at me in shock.

"*You* want to be on the show?" he asked.

The truth was I was scared to death to be on

the show. But the idea of winning all that money was so tempting.

Money had been scarce around our house for the last few years. I tried to help out by mowing yards. In a good week, I could make $100.

But if I won the game, I could contribute a lot more. After all, I was the man of the house now. It was my responsibility.

"T. J.!" Douglas shouted at me.

"Just a minute!" I yelled back. "I'm still thinking about it."

"Well, think about this," Douglas said, grinning. "All you have to do is call the 800 number and answer 10 questions. If you get them all right, they'll pay your way to New York City to be on the show."

"Okay," I declared. "I'm going to try it."

Once again, Douglas stared at me in shock.

"You're really going to do it?" he asked, wide-eyed.

"Just bring me the phone," I instructed.

I took my time cleaning the butter from my hands. Douglas handed me the phone. I slowly punched in the numbers. My heart beat wildly. I resisted the urge to hang up when I heard it ringing.

I was greeted by a recorded message. Then there was a long explanation about the show.

Finally I was given ten questions to answer. They were multiple choice. I had to push 1, 2, or 3 for my answer.

Suddenly my stomach felt queasy. I didn't know if it was from being nervous or from watching Douglas. He was pacing back and forth in front of me. He never took his eyes off my face.

The first three questions were simple. I began to relax. The next three were a little harder. But I was pretty confident about the answers. After that, they got really hard. I began to get queasy again.

Then came the final question. It was a sports question. Immediately I relaxed. After all, anyone would agree that I was a sports expert. I punched in the answer and waited.

In just a few seconds, the recording said, "Congratulations! You have answered all ten questions correctly!"

"I did it!" I yelled.

"That's so cool!" Douglas cheered. "My best friend is going to be a contestant on *Whiz Kid*!"

"Please stay on the line. One of our representatives will get your name and information," the recording continued.

"Quiet down!" I ordered. "I have to give her my information."

"Hello and congratulations," said a young woman. "You've just won the chance to be a contestant on *Whiz Kid.*"

My voice was trembling as I gave her my name, address, and phone number. She said someone would contact my mom the next day to make arrangements. Then she congratulated me again.

I thought I was going to pass out! But before I could, Douglas was shouting again.

"You really did it!" he hollered. "My best friend did it!"

"Did what?" Mom asked as she came around the corner. "What's all the noise about?"

"Mom!" I yelled. I tripped over the coffee table to get to her. "I just tried out to be on *Whiz Kid*, and I did it! I got all ten answers correct! I won a trip for two to New York City to appear on the show!"

"A trip to New York City?" she asked. She looked suspicious.

I filled her in on all the details.

"They're going to call you tomorrow to make arrangements," I finished.

"Well, it sounds wonderful. But don't get too excited until I find out the details and make sure it's for real," Mom warned.

"I won't," I promised. But inside I was already planning my trip to New York.

"Everyone is going to be so jealous," Douglas said. "I can't wait to tell—"

"Hold on a minute," I interrupted. "I think we should keep it a secret for a while. Only you, my mom, and my sister can know for now."

"What?" he asked in disbelief. "I want to tell *everybody*. This is the biggest thing that's ever happened to anyone from Granger City."

"It just feels too good to be true," I tried to explain. "I think we should keep quiet for now. At least until they call back tomorrow and everything is set. I don't want to do anything to jinx it."

"Okay, T. J.," Douglas whined. "But it's going to be awfully tough to keep it a secret."

"It's just for a day," I said. "It won't be that hard for one day."

I soon found out that it wasn't going to be *hard* to keep a secret in Granger City. It was going to be *impossible*!

2

The Secret Is Out

I awoke the next morning with a start. What if it had all been a dream? Maybe I wasn't really going to be on *Whiz Kid*. I sat up and scanned my room for any sign that it was true.

Before any serious panic set in, Alexis came bounding into my room. She jumped right in the middle of my bed.

"Hey, whiz kid!" she greeted.

I plopped back down on the pillow in relief. It really *was* true!

"When did you get to be so smart?" she teased.

"I don't know." I smiled. "I'm just as surprised as you."

"I never dreamed my little brother would be good for my social life," she said.

"What are you talking about?" I asked.

"You're going to be big news at the high school today," she explained. "Everyone will be asking about T. J. Westin."

I sat up again and grabbed her arm.

"No!" I shouted as I squeezed her arm.

"What's wrong with you?" she asked, shaking off my grip.

"I want to keep it a secret," I pleaded. "Just until everything is set. I don't want to do anything to jinx it."

"That's silly," she laughed. "You can't jinx it by talking about it."

"Even so," I said seriously, "I want to keep it a secret for today. We can tell everyone tomorrow."

"Yeah, sure," she said, chuckling. "Whatever."

14

I had serious doubts that Alexis would keep it a secret. In fact, I wasn't sure she *could* keep a secret!

I didn't have any more time to worry about it. I had to get ready for school.

Douglas was ringing the doorbell before I finished getting dressed. I was still buttoning my shirt as I ran down the stairs.

"Hey, whiz kid!" he shouted.

"Don't say that so loud," I complained.

"Oh, yeah," he whispered. "It's a secret."

Then he burst out laughing. I knew I was going to have a hard time keeping him in line.

"You guys better get going," Mom said. She handed me money for lunch.

"Now, Mom," I said. "Remember that you can't leave the house all day. If you do, you might miss the call about the show."

"Today is my day off," she assured me. "You have nothing to worry about. I'll be home all day."

"Are you sure you won't have to leave for anything?" I asked.

"I already promised you three times," she said, pushing me out the door.

"But you can't leave—even for a few minutes," I pressed on. "In fact, don't even go out in the garage. You can't always hear the phone ringing from there."

"Don't worry," she said, getting annoyed now. "I promise I won't leave this house all day."

Still, I watched to make sure she went back into the house before I left. Douglas jabbered all the way to school. He seemed to be more excited about the show than I was. I wouldn't allow myself to get too excited yet. If it all fell through, it would be so disappointing.

I tried to keep to myself at school. If I wasn't around anyone, I wouldn't be tempted to tell.

On the way to class, I passed Shannon Smith's locker. She was standing in a circle with her friends. They were talking and laughing. As I passed them, Shannon stopped talking and smiled at me.

I was so shocked that I forgot to smile back. I'd had a crush on her for two years, but she never seemed to notice. She'd been too busy chasing after Wade Elliott.

I couldn't wait to see Douglas at lunch so I could brag about it. We had our own table in the cafeteria. We sat there every day. But when I entered the room, he wasn't there. It was unusual for him to be late.

I was heading toward our table when I heard my name.

"Hey, T. J.!" Douglas called from the other side of the room. "I saved you a place over here!"

I was shocked to see him with Chad and Rick. They were the most popular guys in school. When I got to their table, they moved down so I could sit with them.

"Hey, T. J.," they said.

"Hey," I said, smiling.

"What's going on?" I whispered to Douglas. "How did you get in with these guys?"

"I didn't do anything," he whispered. He shrugged innocently.

I decided I didn't care. I was just going to enjoy it. First Shannon had smiled at me. Now we were sitting at the cool table. It was the best day I'd had at school for a long time.

I figured my good day would be over when I got to math class. I had forgotten to do my homework because of all the excitement the day before. Usually that means a certain F. But Mrs. White smiled and said she'd allow me to turn it in the next day. Although I was relieved, I thought it was very strange.

The day seemed to pass quickly. I only had one more class to go. Then I could go home and see if anyone had called.

I was on my way to English when I saw Shannon again.

"Hi, T. J.," she said. She flashed me a bright smile.

I smiled back this time. But I couldn't seem to make words come out of my mouth.

"Are you on your way to English?" she asked.

"Uh—yeah," I stuttered.

"Do you mind if I walk with you?" she asked.

"No," I said. *Of course* I don't mind, I thought.

My face felt hot. I knew it was red as we walked down the hall together.

"So what have you been up to?" she asked.

"Not much," I answered.

"I can come over and help you study sometime if you'd like," she offered.

"Is there a big test coming up?" I asked, confused.

"No," she said. "I just thought you might want to do some extra studying."

I was getting more confused by the minute. But then I realized I didn't care what she was talking about. At least she was talking to me.

"I'm in the Honors Club," she said. "You should see about joining too. I'm sure you could be a member."

"Me?" I asked in shock. "In the Honors Club?"

"We could all help you study," she offered. "Then when you go to New York—"

Suddenly it all became clear. My secret wasn't a secret anymore. Douglas had squealed!

"Excuse me," I said, pushing past her.

I tried to catch Douglas, but he was already in history class. I raced to my English class. Luckily, I slipped quietly into the room just as the bell rang.

All through class, my anger grew. As soon as class was over, I charged out the door to find Douglas. I found him huddled with the guys from lunch.

"Hey, Douglas!" I said, pulling him away from the others.

"What's going on?" Douglas complained. "I was talking to the guys."

"I'm the one who wants to know what's going on," I said angrily. "You told, didn't you?"

He opened his mouth to protest. Then he closed it. I guess he knew it was useless to deny it.

"It's okay if everyone knows," Douglas tried to explain. "They're all happy for you."

"But I asked you not to tell," I said. "This could jinx the whole thing."

"I'm telling you it's going to be okay," he said. He followed me to my locker. "It's not going to jinx anything. Wait and see."

"You wait and see," I said, heading out of school. "If something happens, it will be your fault."

We took off on our bikes as fast as we could pedal. When we got to my house, I squealed to a stop. But this time, I didn't bother to check the skid mark. I had more important things to do.

Douglas followed me into the house.

"Mom!" I hollered. "Where are you?"

"I'm right here," she said, coming out of the kitchen. "I thought I'd bake a cake to celebrate."

"To *celebrate*?" I said. "Does that mean what I think it means?"

"Yep," she said, beaming. "It's all set. We're going to New York City!"

3

Having Doubts

Douglas and I started our celebration with a big piece of lemon cake. Alexis came home from school just in time to join us. As I suspected, she hadn't kept the secret either. It was beginning to look like everyone in town already knew. Now *I* was dying to tell somebody—anybody!

My first call was to my number one fan—my grandpa. Just as I figured, he was as excited as I was.

Since Dad had passed away, Grandpa tried to do all the things Dad would have done. He took me fishing and camping at Horseshoe Lake. He never missed one of my baseball games. He even went to all my school activities. I could tell him secrets just like a friend. He was the best grandpa ever.

Next I called all the guys on my baseball team. I even called Coach White and told him the news.

I continued to call everyone I could think of. Finally Mom said that was enough. I sat back in the chair and took a deep breath. I suddenly remembered that I hadn't told Douglas about Shannon.

"Hey, Douglas—" I started.

"He's not here," Mom said. "He left about 30 minutes ago."

"He did?" I asked, surprised. "I guess he had to be home for dinner."

"That reminds me—you need to get started on your homework before we have dinner," Mom said.

"Okay," I said cheerfully. Even homework didn't sound so bad right now. "I'm on my way."

22

I took the stairs two at a time. Jogging into my room, I plopped on the bed. I stretched out and put my hands behind my head. I wanted a few minutes to reflect on my awesome day. Then I'd start my homework.

I closed my eyes and replayed the day. I smiled when I remembered hanging out with Chad and Rick at lunch. I smiled even bigger when I remembered my conversation with Shannon. Being on TV was really going to improve my social life!

It was hard to believe I was actually going to be on a TV show. I wondered if they would insist on putting makeup on me. I'd heard they did that even on the guys. I would definitely refuse that!

It was also hard to believe that I was going to New York City. I'd always thought my first visit there would be when I played for the New York Yankees. But the Yankees would just have to wait for a few years. T. J. Westin was going to be a TV star!

I tried to imagine myself standing onstage playing the game. The TV camera would zoom in on me. I would smile brightly. Then they would zoom in on my opponent. That would probably be some brainy girl who was president of the science club.

Then they would ask the question. Of course I would hit the buzzer first. The camera would zoom in on me again. I would look directly into the camera and . . . and . . .

I sat up quickly and looked around the room nervously. Suddenly I felt the urge to hide somewhere. What had I done?

What if the camera zoomed in on me and my mind went completely blank? Or even worse, I might give the wrong answer. The girl would buzz in and get the answer right. I would look like an idiot!

Suddenly my mind was swirling with doubts. I remembered my last report card. I pictured the C in English. Even though I mostly made As and Bs, I also got an occasional C. What had I been thinking? I wasn't smart enough to be on *Whiz Kid*!

But wait, I thought. I could study really hard. We didn't leave until Monday. I still had five days. But then I realized that five days wasn't very long.

I felt a full-blown panic attack coming on. Luckily, I was interrupted by the phone.

"T. J., the phone's for you!" Alexis yelled.

"Tell him I'm not here," I called back. There was no way I could speak to anyone. I was in the middle of a crisis.

"Are you sure?" Alexis asked. She stuck her head around the door. "It's a girl."

"A girl?" I asked, snapping out of my crisis.

"She says her name is Shannon," Alexis said.

"Shannon?" I asked in surprise.

"Why's a girl calling you anyway?" Alexis asked as she followed me down the hall.

"None of your business," I muttered as I ran for the phone.

"Shannon?" I asked. I pressed the phone tightly against my ear. I didn't want any sound to leak out so Alexis could hear.

"Hey, T. J.!" Shannon said happily. "What are you doing?"

"Nothing much," I said. I didn't think she'd be very impressed with a guy who was scared out of his wits.

"I just wanted to remind you that I'll help you study," she said. "If you need me to."

"That would be great," I said nervously. "Maybe we could do that tomorrow after school."

I'd had as much excitement as I could stand for one day. I just couldn't cope with trying to impress Shannon any more today.

We agreed to meet in the library after school tomorrow. I shuffled back to my room. I pulled back the curtain and gazed out the window. I was lost in thought, not really looking at anything. Suddenly I realized that Mom was standing in the doorway.

"What are you doing?" she asked.

"Nothing," I muttered. I turned back to the window.

"What's wrong?" she asked. "You were so excited before. Now you're so quiet."

I moved to the edge of the bed and sat down. I wasn't quite sure where to start.

"I just wasn't thinking about what was going to happen when I get there," I started.

"What are you talking about?" she asked with a puzzled look.

I hated to say it out loud, but I had to.

"What if I freeze up when they ask me a question?" I asked. "Or even worse, what if I just don't know the answer?"

"T. J.," Mom said. She sat beside me on the bed. "There's one thing I've always known about you. You're a smart kid. You always have been."

"You *have* to say that because you're my mother," I said.

"That's not true," she assured me. "I know you're smart because you're just like your dad. And he was the smartest man I've ever known."

"He was?" I asked in surprise. "Did he get straight As in school?"

"No," she said, laughing. "I don't think so. But getting all As doesn't always measure how smart you are."

"Mrs. Scoggins sure seems to think so," I muttered. Mrs. Scoggins was my English teacher. She always favored the top students.

"Well, this time you listen to *me*," Mom said firmly. "I know that if you do your best, you can win that game."

"I sure hope so," I said.

"You only need to worry about one thing," she added with a smile. "And that's what you'll buy with the money you'll win."

"Thanks, Mom," I said.

"You're welcome. Now come eat your dinner," she said. "I'd like to get finished in the kitchen and go to bed. I have to work the early shift tomorrow. I need to be out of bed by 5:30 a.m."

Mom was a nurse at St. Joseph's Hospital. She made enough money to pay the bills, but there was seldom any money left over. She'd had to work extra shifts last summer to buy a new washing machine. Now the van had been in the shop for a week. I knew she was worried about paying for that.

When I got to the kitchen, Alexis was leaving for drill practice. Then she had a Drama Club meeting. Her schedule was very hectic, but she liked it that way.

Mom and I were both tired. We finished dinner quietly. While she did the dishes, I took out the trash.

I had to struggle to fit it into the plastic trash container. I finally shoved it down with all my strength. The plastic container split open down one side. Trash spilled out all over. I was furious with myself for being in such a hurry. Now we'd have to buy another trash container.

That reminded me why I wanted to win the money so badly. We needed it to fix the van and replace some worn-out things around the house. But most of all, I just wanted to see the surprised look on Mom's face when I handed her the money. If I had to study night and day, that's what I'd do.

4

Study, Study, Study

As soon as I cleaned up the trash, I went straight to my room to study. I dumped out my backpack on the bed. I was hoping I had a book to study with. All I found were a math workbook, some candy papers, a broken pencil, and some dirty socks.

Everything I needed to study with was in my locker at school. Most of my books hadn't seen the inside of my backpack all year.

I always studied hard during class. But I really hated homework. I didn't think there was any need to lug those heavy books home every day.

I worked on a few math problems. Soon I got too sleepy to concentrate. I drifted off to sleep, dreaming of fame and fortune.

I was awake before the alarm went off the next morning. I had my bed made and was already dressed when Grandpa called at 7:00.

"Hey, Grandpa," I said. "What's going on?"

"I'm calling to give you your daily brainteaser," he said.

"What are you talking about?" I asked.

I could imagine Grandpa sitting at his kitchen table. He was probably masterminding some trick question.

"Every morning, I'll call you with a brainteaser," he explained. "This is my way of helping you study. Unless, of course, you're not up to the challenge."

"Okay," I laughed. "Go for it! I'm ready when you are."

"Uh-hum," he said, clearing his throat. "Today's question will be based on geography."

I figured that would be a cinch. Geography and history were my best subjects.

"How many states in the United States begin with the letter M?" he asked. "Name them."

"That's too easy, Grandpa!" I exclaimed.

"No comments, please," he said in a deep voice. "Just answer the question."

I counted on my fingers as I named them.

"Maine, Maryland, Massachusetts, Minnesota, Missouri, Montana, and Michigan," I said with confidence. "There are seven states that start with the letter M."

"Buzzzzz," he said loudly. "That's incorrect. You forgot one."

"No, I didn't," I argued.

"You forgot Mississippi," he said.

"Oh, no," I moaned.

"That's okay, T. J.," he laughed. "You'll have another chance tomorrow!"

As I hung up the phone, I worried. If I couldn't answer Grandpa's questions, how could I answer the show's?

I grabbed an encyclopedia on my way to breakfast. I propped it up behind my bowl of cereal. I figured I would at least know the answers that started with the letter A. I was still studying when Douglas got there.

"That's my buddy, the genius," he said. "Are we going to study together after school?"

"I never got to tell you yesterday," I said excitedly. "Shannon Smith offered to help me study. She's going to meet me in the library after school."

"You're kidding me, right?" he asked in disbelief.

"She even called me last night," I said, grinning. "And she said I could study with the Honors Club."

"The Honors Club?" he shouted. "T. J. Westin in the Honors Club?"

"It sounds pretty bad when you say it like that." I frowned. "But those guys are really smart. They can help me a lot."

"Yeah, I guess so," Douglas said. He was quiet then. I knew what he was thinking. I prided myself in always knowing what Douglas was thinking. Sometimes I knew what he was thinking before he even thought it.

"But you're going with me," I added. "I'm not going unless you go too."

Douglas's face brightened as he shook his head in agreement.

"Okay," he said.

Normally we hung around the house until the very last minute. We had it timed so we could slide into our seats, count to five, and the bell would ring.

But today we were out the door way before 8:00. I needed to find my books, so Douglas helped me clean out my locker. We stuffed all the books into my backpack. I was hoping some of that knowledge would seep into my brain while I carried them around.

Then we began on the junk at the bottom of the locker. A strange smell had been wafting from my locker for a couple of weeks.

"That's the last thing," Douglas said. He pointed to a green object. "I'm not touching it."

I pinched my nose and reached for the object. Just moving it around caused the smell to get stronger. We weren't sure what it was. I decided I didn't want to know. I dumped it in the garbage can down the hall. That way no one would know it belonged to me.

Just as I was closing the locker, Shannon appeared behind me.

"Are we still going to study after school?" she asked.

"Uh—yeah," I stammered.

"Maybe I'll see you at lunch too," she said as she disappeared into math class.

"I think she's in love," Douglas teased as he followed me down the hall.

I didn't let his teasing get to me. I went straight to class. I was anxious to soak up as much wisdom as possible.

During the day, I set up a schedule for studying. My teachers even offered tutoring in the mornings before school.

I decided I should work the hardest on my weakest subjects. Those would definitely be science and English. I accepted Mr. Richardson's offer for science tutoring on Thursday morning. I also agreed to meet with Mrs. Scoggins for English on Friday.

After school, I would meet with the Honors Club. At night, I would study on my own. Douglas would help me on the weekend.

It was an exhausting schedule. But I only had five days to prepare. And I needed to study as much as possible.

My only free time was lunch. Shannon met me at the cafeteria every day. We sat with Rick and Chad at the popular table.

I was doing a good job of sticking to my hectic schedule until Friday evening. That's when Chad invited us to come to his house to study. At first I resisted the change in my schedule. But I finally decided that it would be a good break.

Douglas and I weren't prepared for the size of Chad's house. I knew that all the homes in the Treasure Hills subdivision were supposed to be nice.

But I'd never been in a house like his before.

His bedroom was like a dream room. He had his own telephone, an entertainment center with hundreds of CDs, and a new computer.

For the first time, I was embarrassed about where I lived. I'd never let that kind of thing bother me before. But I'd never seen a house like Chad's before either.

Everyone seemed to forget that we were supposed to study. Chad was busy showing off his newest toy—a DVD player. Rick suggested we try it out and watch a movie.

Shannon was paying more attention to me than ever. I was having a great time. And I was thrilled to take a break from studying.

"Let's get out of here," Douglas whispered. "We can go to my house and study."

"Are you crazy?" I asked. "I'm staying here."

"You made me promise to help you stay on schedule," he reminded me. He picked up my backpack and headed to the door.

"Sorry, but we have to go," he told the others.

I was so furious that I refused to move. I just stood there staring at him. After a few moments, he turned and left. I followed him out the door, but I wasn't happy about it. We didn't talk again until we got to his house. As soon as we got to his room, I let him have it.

"I don't need a baby-sitter, you know!" I said angrily.

"What's the matter with you?" he shouted. "I'm trying to help."

"You're just butting in!" I yelled. "You're just jealous because I have new friends now—popular, rich friends!"

I could see in his eyes that I'd hurt him. I wasn't even sure why I'd said it. It was stupid.

"Just go home," Douglas said quietly.

"I'm sorry," I said. "You know I didn't mean that."

He opened the door and stood there. He was waiting for me to leave. I slowly picked up my backpack and walked out of his room.

I had plenty of time to think on the walk home. In the last week, my whole life had changed. I was stressed-out and exhausted. Only two more days remained before I left for New York City. Maybe trying out for *Whiz Kid* had been a big mistake.

5

Encouraging Words

Saturday morning, Douglas appeared at my door right on schedule. After our fight, I'd been afraid he wouldn't show up. I was relieved to see him. He was quieter than usual, but neither of us mentioned the argument again.

The next two days passed too quickly. Before I knew it, I was packing for the trip. We had to be at the airport in Austin at 6:00 a.m. The plane was leaving at 7:00. Mom insisted we get there an hour early.

Mom had changed her schedule so she would be off work for three days. We made a list of places we wanted to see while we were in New York City. We were hoping I would at least win the first game. Then we could stay an extra day.

It seemed as if everyone I knew called to wish me good luck. Chad and Rick called Sunday afternoon. Shannon called twice just to say good-bye. Each of the guys on the baseball team called. Even Coach White called to give me a pep talk.

"You're a smart guy, T. J.," he said. "I know you can do this. Just concentrate and focus on the question."

"I'll do my best, Coach," I promised.

"The whole team is behind you," he said. "I'm taking a TV set to the gym. We're all going to watch the show together."

A reporter even came and took my picture for the *Granger City News*. He said he was writing an article about my appearance on the show. I'd never had my picture in the newspaper before.

Grandpa showed up Sunday evening with two large pizzas for dinner.

"T. J. told me once that pizza increases blood flow to the brain," Grandpa explained. "I figure it's worth a try."

"I believe T. J. says that about all his favorite foods," Mom said, laughing.

I called Douglas and he came over and had pizza with us. I was relieved that he was acting normal again.

"I have a final brainteaser for you," Grandpa said.

"Okay," I laughed. "Let me have it."

"Who was Nolan Ryan's five thousandth strikeout?" he asked.

"I know who it is," I said. "But I can't remember his name."

"Oh—oh—I know!" Douglas shouted.

"Don't say it," Grandpa warned Douglas.

"I can picture him in my mind, but I can't think of his name!" I groaned.

"I need an answer by the time I count to five," Grandpa pressed. "One—two—three—"

"Rickey Henderson!" I screamed.

"Right!" Grandpa said. "And just before the buzzer."

We sat around the table talking and laughing for two hours. Finally, Mom insisted we break it up and get to bed.

I walked outside with Douglas when he was leaving.

"Good luck." Douglas slapped me on the back. "You're going to win. I know you are."

"Thanks for helping me study all week," I said. "And for keeping me on my schedule," I added. "I really appreciate it."

"No problem," he said as he jumped on his bike. "Just don't forget everything I taught you!"

I started back into the house. Grandpa met me at the front door. He slung his arm over my shoulders and turned me around. We walked back down the front walk.

"You must be tired," he said. "You've really worked hard this week."

"Not really," I said, shaking my head. "I'm actually kind of pumped up. I probably won't be able to sleep tonight."

"You're going to do great," he assured me. "Sleep well and don't worry about a thing."

Then he turned me to face him. His steel blue eyes were surrounded by soft wrinkles.

"I'm proud of you," he said seriously. "And your dad would be really proud of you too."

"Thanks for saying that, Grandpa," I said quietly. "That's good to hear."

He hugged me quickly and walked to his car. I thought about how hard it must have been for him to lose his son. I knew he still missed Dad—maybe as much as I did.

Tears sprang to my eyes as I thought about Dad. I could barely remember him when he wasn't sick. The disease had slowly robbed him of his strength. At first, he'd been able to walk with a cane. Then he'd used a wheelchair. In the end, he'd had to stay in bed.

He'd never complained about anything. Whenever I came home from school, he was always waiting for me with a smile. I'd tell him all about my day. He'd make me laugh so much that sometimes I forgot he was even sick.

It was times like these that I missed him the most. I had so much I wanted to tell him.

I went back upstairs and did a final check of my suitcase. I knew I was just stalling. I didn't want to go to bed. It was unlikely that I'd be able to sleep anyway.

I decided to prop up in bed with my English book. It wouldn't hurt to look through it one more time. But sleep came much easier than I'd thought it would. Before I knew it, the alarm sounded.

I opened my eyes and stretched lazily. I glanced around the room. Why was it so dark at 7:00 in the morning? I looked at the alarm clock. It was only 4:30. That's when I remembered! This was the big day!

I jumped out of bed and started grabbing my clothes. I dressed, made my bed, and carried my suitcase downstairs in less than ten minutes. Whew! I was going to have to slow down or I was going to kill myself!

Mom and I ate a quick bowl of cereal. Then Grandpa showed up to take us to the airport. Since we arrived at 6:00, we had an hour to wait. Grandpa and I paced back and forth in front of the big windows facing the airfield. It wasn't long before Mom was pacing with us. I wasn't sure who was more nervous—me or them!

We watched our plane pull up to the gate. Grandpa wished me luck one more time. Finally we boarded the plane. Mom gave me the window seat since it was my first time flying.

It was such a rush when the plane lifted off the ground. Minutes later, we were in the clouds. The sun was rising. It was going to be a beautiful day.

I sat back and smiled broadly.

"Look out New York City!" I said quietly. "Tanner James Westin is on his way!"

6

An Exciting
First Day

When we arrived at the New York City airport, we panicked. We'd never seen so many people in one place. We were relieved when a man in a dark suit approached us. He would be our driver while we were here. He helped us get our luggage and took us to the car. It was a white limousine!

Mom and I laughed and talked excitedly as we were driven through the city.

"We'll be at the studio in just a few minutes," the driver told us.

I stopped laughing. My nervousness grew as I remembered why I was really in New York City. The rest of the ride was quiet.

When we arrived at the studio, everyone was friendly. They placed Mom in a chair behind the cameraman. I was relieved I could see her clearly in case I needed some moral support.

Just as I had feared, a woman came around with a tray of makeup.

"I'm sure I don't need that," I announced.

"Just a little powder to take away the shine," she said. "You can't go on TV with a shine on your face."

Before I could stop her, my nose had been powdered and she had disappeared.

Russ Connor came over and introduced himself. He seemed very nice. I began to calm down.

That didn't last long though. It all changed when I met my opponent.

"This is Amanda Brinkley," Russ said.

"How do you do?" she asked formally.

I was sure I was staring into the face of a girl who'd gotten straight As since kindergarten.

Everything about her was perfect—her hair, her clothes, even her teeth!

She took her place next to me. We each had a buzzer in front of us. Once we were set, the cameras moved into place.

The stage seemed as if it were shrinking. I felt as if I were choking. I tried to adjust my collar. I used my hand to wipe the sweat off my forehead. Oh, no! Now I had a shiny face!

While I was panicking, the music began playing. Russ walked toward the camera with his microphone. He smiled as he waited for his cue.

"Good afternoon, everybody!" he greeted. "Welcome to *Whiz Kid*! On the left, we have our returning champion, Amanda Brinkley."

I watched as the camera zoomed in on Amanda's perfect, smiling face.

"Amanda is in the seventh grade at Washington Junior High in Oklahoma City," he continued. "She's won the President's Award for academic achievement for the last two years."

I knew it! My opponent was a genius!

"And on the right, we have our challenger, T. J. Westin," he said loudly.

I froze as I watched the camera zoom in on my face. I could only hope that it was so shiny that no one would recognize me.

"T. J. is a seventh grader at Granger Middle School in Granger City, Texas," he said. "He's a member of the Granger Warriors baseball team."

I could feel the heat in my face. I knew I was as red as a tomato. Everyone was probably laughing at me.

Russ read the rules for the game. There would be 21 questions worth $100 apiece. Then the winner would receive a bonus question worth $2,000. He wished us both luck.

I swallowed hard, squared my shoulders, and stood tall. For some reason, it gave me comfort to know that even if I wasn't smart, I was tall.

"Here's the first question," Russ said. "In what year did women get the right to vote?"

I started to hit the buzzer but paused for just a second.

"Yes, Amanda," Russ was saying.

"The year was 1920," she said brightly.

I was furious with myself. I knew that answer. Douglas and I had gone over it just a couple of days ago.

I took a deep breath. I tried to imagine that I was in my living room with Douglas. Sitting in front of me was my popcorn and soda. Then I leaned closer to the buzzer and steadied myself for the next question.

"What is the name of the game played in England that is similar to American football?" Russ asked.

I knew everything about sports. This was a cinch. I hit the buzzer so hard that Russ jumped.

"Yes, T. J.?" he asked.

"The answer is rugby," I said confidently.

"That's right!" he exclaimed. "The score is 1 to 1."

"This is the third question," said Russ. "In 1963, President John F. Kennedy was assassinated. In what city did this take place?"

I hit the buzzer again.

"Yes, T. J.?" asked Russ.

"The city was Dallas, Texas," I said, smiling.

"That's correct," he said.

I was feeling much better now. I glanced quickly at Amanda. I was sure I saw some sweat on her forehead. That gave me even more confidence.

From then on, no matter what the question was, the answer would pop into my head immediately. It wasn't long before Russ was announcing the winner.

"We have a final score of 2 for Amanda," he said, "and 19 for T. J. That makes T. J. Westin our new champion! He'll take home $1,900. He'll also have a chance at the bonus question. If he's able to answer it correctly, he can win another $2,000."

My head was spinning. I was glad he didn't give me any time to think about it. He went right into the bonus round.

"Okay, T. J.," Douglas said seriously. "This is your bonus question. President Abraham Lincoln was remembered for many things. But he is perhaps best known for a document that he signed in 1863. Can you tell me the name of this document?"

"The document is the Emancipation Proclamation," I said.

"You're right!" Russ exclaimed. "You've won a total of $3,900!"

Then he turned to the camera and announced, "Be sure to tune in tomorrow. Our champion, T. J. Westin, will be back to face a new challenger!"

I was grinning so hard my face hurt. Everyone shook my hand and congratulated me. Mom was so excited that her hands were trembling. We talked to the producer for a few minutes about the next show.

Afterwards, we were driven to our hotel in the limousine. The hotel was even better than the limo. We felt like royalty when we stepped out of the car in front of the Grand Manhattan Hotel.

I'd only stayed in a hotel room a few times. But I'd never stayed in anything like this before! We had a private balcony with a view of the Manhattan skyline. The beds were huge with thick covers and soft feather pillows. A little refrigerator was packed full of snacks and drinks. The bathroom even had a Jacuzzi.

Mom was overwhelmed with the limousine and the hotel. She kept repeating how beautiful everything was. The last six years had been harder on her than anyone. I was so proud that I'd won the trip. Mom could finally have some fun and be pampered too.

We got all dressed up for dinner that night. We went downstairs to the hotel dining room. It was the fanciest restaurant we'd ever seen. The food was delicious—although I didn't recognize some of it.

When we got back to our room, we were exhausted. I got to try the Jacuzzi first. Then while Mom tried it out, I propped up on the bed and surrounded myself with pillows. The TV had 132 channels. I was having a blast when Grandpa called.

I told him everything about my day. He was thrilled for me.

"I always knew you could do it," he told me. "Just hang in there and you'll win tomorrow too."

"Wouldn't that be great?" I asked. "If I won again, I could double my money!"

Grandpa wished me good luck and said good-bye. I turned off the TV and tried to go to sleep. It wasn't easy though. I kept worrying that winning the first game was just a fluke. What if I couldn't do it again?

T.J. Westin

7

A Star Is Born

The driver delivered us to the studio again the next day. Everyone made us feel welcome. I was really enjoying all the special attention. I didn't even mind getting my face powdered.

Russ introduced the new challenger to me just before the game started. Her name was Courtney Swanson. Her red hair and freckles made her look friendly. But I was still afraid that underneath that ponytail was a superbrain.

The music began. Russ read the rules and made the introductions. I felt a little less nervous than the day before.

"Okay," Russ said. "This is question number one. Spell the word *handkerchief*."

I hit the buzzer, but it was too late. Courtney had beat me to it.

"Go head, Courtney," Russ said.

"*Handkerchief* is spelled h-a-n-d-k-e-r-c-h-e-f," she said.

"I'm sorry," Russ said. "T. J., would you like to try this one?"

"Yes," I said nervously. "It's h-a-n-d-k-e-r-c-h-i-e-f."

"That's correct," Russ said, smiling. "Okay, question number two. What is the capital of Florida?"

She beat me on the buzzer again! That girl sure was fast on the draw!

"The capital of Florida," she said excitedly, "is Miami."

"No, sorry," Russ said. "T. J., do you have an answer?"

"The capital of Florida is Tallahassee," I said calmly.

"Very good!" Russ said.

That's the way the rest of the game went. Even though Courtney beat me on the buzzer sometimes, she usually missed the answer. At the end of the game, the score was 18 to 3. I won again!

"It's time for the bonus question," Russ said. "A correct answer is worth $2,000. Are you ready, T. J.?" he asked.

"I think so," I gulped.

"Then here's the question," he stated. "In what year did the Boston Tea Party take place?"

"The Boston Tea Party took place in 1773," I answered quickly.

"Absolutely right!" Russ declared. "That gives you a total for today of $3,800. Together with yesterday's winnings, you have a grand total of $7,700!"

As soon as the cameras were turned off, Mom came running.

"That was amazing, T. J.!" she exclaimed. "You didn't even have to think about the answers. You just called them out so easily."

"I don't understand it," I tried to explain. "When I start playing, it's like everything I ever learned just pops into my head."

"I'm so proud of you!" Mom said happily.

The producer came over and congratulated me again. We made plans to be back for the show the next day. Then Mom and I set out to explore New York City.

We spent several hours at the Museum of Modern Art. We bought some T-shirts for Alexis and Douglas. Then we went to Times Square.

As soon as we got back to the hotel room, I called Douglas. Mom had said no long-distance phone calls at first. But now that I'd won so much money, she didn't argue.

"That is so awesome!" Douglas howled. "You're going to win again tomorrow. I know you will!"

"Maybe," I said, grinning into the phone.

I didn't give him much of a chance to tell me what was going on back home. Instead I told him every detail of my trip. I described the limo and the hotel. I told him everything we'd seen in New York City.

"Call me again tomorrow," he said. "I want to hear everything!"

I promised I would and said good-bye. Then I called Grandpa. I told him the whole story over again.

When we finally went to bed at 10:30, my body was exhausted. My mind, however, was still reeling. I just couldn't believe that something so wonderful was happening to me. I was almost afraid to go to sleep. I was afraid I would wake up and it would all be a dream.

When I woke up the next morning, I opened my eyes slowly. I smiled when I realized I was still in that luxurious hotel.

A while later, the driver called to tell us he had arrived to take us to the studio. Life was so good!

My opponent for the third day was a girl named Brooke Harper. I was feeling a little more confident by then, so she didn't worry me much. She beat me to the buzzer a few times. But whenever I got to the buzzer first, I always came up with the right answer.

I won 17 to 4. That meant another $1,700. Then came the bonus question.

"Okay, T. J.," Russ said. "This is your bonus question. Are invertebrates animals with or without a backbone?"

I almost smirked at how simple the question was.

"Russ, an invertebrate is an animal without a backbone," I declared.

"Right again!" he shouted. "That means your total for today is $3,700. That brings your grand total to $11,400!"

It was such a rush to know I'd won all that money. I decided it was time to enjoy some of it.

"Three wins in a row!" Mom was gushing. "That means we have another day to spend in New York City. Where should we go today?"

"I'd like to go shopping," I stated firmly.

"*Shopping*?" Mom exclaimed. "*You* want to go *shopping*?"

"I can't keep wearing the same clothes on TV every day," I pointed out. "Besides, I could get some really cool clothes here."

Still in shock, Mom agreed to a shopping trip. We hailed a taxi and headed to Bloomingdale's. We spent the whole afternoon picking out new clothes. Mom would only agree to buy one new dress for herself. She insisted I spend the money on myself.

I, on the other hand, purchased a whole new wardrobe. I bought all the brand-name clothes we couldn't afford before.

We got back to the hotel late that night. I was too tired to call Douglas. I decided I would talk to him in a day or so.

✝ ✝ ✝ ✝ ✝ ✝ ✝ ✝ ✝

The next two days were easy wins. At the end of my five-day winning streak, I had a total of $18,800.

After the fifth show, the producer called Mom and me into his office.

"I want to congratulate you, T. J.," he started. "You're the first contestant on our show to win five times in a row."

"Thank you," I said proudly.

"I also need to remind you about the rules of the game," he continued. "We'll only allow you to play seven games in a row. If you win seven times, you'll have to step down. We'll bring in a new player."

"Oh, okay," I said quietly, trying to hide my disappointment.

"But we'll sure hate to see you go," the producer added. "You've been great for our ratings. Yesterday's ratings for the show were the highest ever.

"In fact," the producer added, "we'll be putting some extra commercial spots on. We have confidence that you will play all seven games. So we'll be putting your picture in some ads for the show."

"You might want to watch for yourself on TV," the producer said to me. "We'll run the ads through the weekend."

As soon as our meeting was over, Mom and I headed straight for the hotel. I positioned myself on the bed with the remote. I knew which channels would air the commercial spots. I clicked back and forth between the channels the rest of the day. Mom and I cheered every time I appeared.

The clips showed me answering the bonus questions. I was impressed that I didn't even look nervous.

"Will T. J. Westin be the first to win seven times in a row?" the announcer asked. "Tune in to *Whiz Kid* on Monday to find out."

I couldn't believe it! I was a TV star!

8

The Champion

    I wanted to stay in the hotel room all weekend.
I didn't want to miss any of my commercials. But
Mom insisted that we go sightseeing.

She got a map of New York City, and we took off walking. First we went to the Empire State Building. We rode up to the observation deck. The view was awesome.

We also spent a lot of time in Central Park. It was green and full of trees. It was hard to believe we were in the middle of all those skyscrapers.

We stopped at a street vendor on the way back to the hotel and bought hot dogs. As we ate, we watched the crowds passing by. Mom and I laughed at some of the interesting people. We definitely weren't in Granger City anymore!

On Sunday, we decided to visit the Statue of Liberty. We had to ride the subway to Battery Park. We were scared at first. In Granger City, we only had one bus for public transportation. And it was never this crowded!

We made it safely to Battery Park. Then we took a boat to Liberty Island. An elevator took us to the foot of the statue. From there we had a cool view of the harbor and the city. Then we climbed a steep, narrow, spiral staircase to the statue's crown. Mom was exhausted from the climb, but I thought it was fun.

We were also able to tour Ellis Island. It had been a U.S. immigration station for over 60 years. Now it had been restored and was open to the public.

No matter where we went, I thought about the game. I couldn't really concentrate on any of the sights. I forgot about everything and everyone else—including Douglas and Grandpa. I didn't call either all weekend.

I just wanted to get on with the winning. I was enjoying my newfound popularity. I was so glad when Monday finally arrived.

I made it through the sixth show without any problems. The final score was 18 to 3. Then I answered the bonus question correctly. My total winnings for that day were $3,800.

Now all I had to do was win that all-important seventh game.

Tuesday morning, I dressed in one of my new outfits. I even took a little extra time with my hair. I wanted to look my best for my last appearance.

I strolled out of the hotel and stepped into the limousine. I was more confident than I'd ever been. I wasn't even thinking about the money anymore. I only cared about one thing now. I wanted the glory!

When we arrived at the studio, everyone was rushing around. I was immediately taken aside by the assistant. She wanted to recomb my hair, but I refused. I was sure it was perfect.

I no longer minded the makeup lady. In fact, I urged her to apply extra powder. A lot of people would be watching the show. I didn't want to get caught with a shine on my nose.

I was checking myself out in the mirror when Mom came looking for me.

"I just came to wish you luck," Mom said, giving me a hug.

"Watch the hair, Mom!" I complained.

"Only two minutes until we're on the air, T. J.," said the assistant.

"I have to get going, Mom," I said as I brushed past her.

I took my place onstage. I made sure I was standing just right for the cameras. Russ brought the new opponent over to make a quick introduction.

"Hi," she said shyly. "My name is Emily Liu."

"Nice to meet you," I said curtly, nodding my head slightly.

We took our places and the music started. Russ went through his usual introduction and rules. Finally he came to the first question.

"This is the first question for $100," Russ said. "What are the three branches of the American government?"

I hit the buzzer first and smiled confidently.

"Yes, T. J.?" Russ said.

"The three branches of the American government are the executive, legislative, and judicial."

"That's correct," Russ declared. "Now for question number two. Who was the author of *The Adventures of Tom Sawyer*?"

Once again, I hit the buzzer first with the correct answer—Mark Twain.

I glanced over at Emily. I expected to see her cowering in the corner. To my surprise, she was leaning over the desk. Her hand was poised over the buzzer.

"Question number three will be a true/false question," Russ instructed. "An equilateral triangle has all three sides of the same length. True or false?"

Emily whacked the buzzer so hard that it could be heard throughout the studio.

"The answer is true," she said quickly.

"That's correct!" Russ smiled. "Question number four," he continued. "Name three of the five Great Lakes."

Emily slammed the buzzer again.

"Lake Erie, Lake Huron, and Lake Superior," she said brightly.

"That's absolutely correct," Russ said. "Question number five. Who was the commander of the Confederate Army?"

I was determined to get to the buzzer first this time. But Emily beat me again!

"The Commander of the Confederate Army

was Robert E. Lee," she said happily.

"Correct once again," Russ said.

I couldn't figure out what was going on. Things were getting out of hand. She was actually beating me! I had to get back in control of the game!

"Question number six," Russ said. "What is the name of the center of a cell—also called the cell's control center?"

Bam! I hit the buzzer with so much force that Russ stopped and frowned at me.

"Yes, T. J.?" he asked.

"The center of a cell is the nucleus," I said quickly.

"That's correct," he said, still not smiling. "That makes the score three to three. What is the name of the mythical creature that is half-horse and half-fish?"

Bam! Both buzzers sounded.

"The answer is a sea horse!" Emily shouted.

"You might want to lighten up on those buzzers a bit," Russ suggested as he looked at both of us.

There was no way I was going to lighten up. Emily remained hovering over her buzzer too. It was going to be a battle to the very end!

The next ten questions were a blur. We went back and forth answering the questions. When we got to question 18, Emily was 1 ahead of me.

That's when I decided enough was enough. I gathered up every ounce of strength I had and waited for the next question.

"It's a close game," Russ was saying. "And here's question number 18. In what year did the Pilgrims land at Plymouth?"

Bam! I hit the buzzer as hard as I could. I didn't care what Russ thought.

"The answer is 1620," I said.

"Correct," Russ said. "Question number 19. What is the capital of Pennsylvania?"

Whack! Emily beat me again!

"The answer is Philadelphia," she said quickly.

"I'm sorry," Russ said. "That's incorrect. T. J., would you like to try?"

"The answer is Harrisburg," I answered.

"Correct," he declared. "Now the twentieth question. Which amendment to the Constitution outlawed slavery?"

Bam! Emily got it!

"The Thirteenth Amendment outlawed slavery," she said.

"That's correct!" Russ exclaimed. "That means the game is tied ten to ten! The final question will decide the winner!"

I glared at Emily. She glared right back at me. She was a tough opponent!

"Question number 21," Russ said slowly and clearly. "The smallest bones in your body are found where?"

I knew the answer! I just couldn't remember what it was! I had just studied it in science class with Mr. Richardson. For a brief second, I panicked. I couldn't come up with the answer. Then suddenly I remembered! I hit the buzzer loudly.

"Yes, T. J.?" Russ asked.

"The smallest bones in your body are found in the ear," I said proudly.

"Correct!" Russ yelled.

The bonus question passed in a blur. I don't even remember answering it. The next thing I knew music was playing loudly.

"T. J. Westin has won seven games in a row!" Russ announced.

Confetti fell from the ceiling. The crew cheered and Mom came running.

"T. J. has set a record on our show," Russ was saying. "Never before have we had a contestant win seven games in a row! According to the rules of *Whiz Kid*, he'll be stepping down. However, he'll take with him today's winnings of $3,100 and his grand total of $25,700!"

Once the cameras were off, everyone gathered around me. They congratulated me, patting me on the back. After a while, Mom pulled me away from the crowd.

"I've arranged for a flight home later this afternoon," she whispered. "We need to pick up our things at the hotel and head to the airport."

"No, Mom," I argued. "Let's stay another day."

"I really need to get back to work," she said. "I've been gone much longer than I'd planned."

I didn't see much point in arguing about it. She'd obviously made up her mind.

I soaked up my last few minutes of attention. We cherished our last limousine ride to the hotel and then to the airport.

When we boarded the plane, I began to get excited about going home. I was sure everyone would be anxious to see me. They would probably have lots of questions to ask me. After all, I was a *Whiz Kid* champion and rich TV star.

9

The Biggest
Jerk in the World

When I entered the airport terminal in Austin, lights began flashing all around me. I heard voices calling my name. A group of people with cameras and notepads stood nearby. I realized it was a group of reporters waiting for me. It just proved that I was definitely a big star now.

"T. J.!" one man was calling. "Tell us how it felt to be a seven-time winner on *Whiz Kid*!"

"It wasn't as hard as I thought it would be," I replied. "The questions seemed kind of easy."

"Do you think you could ever do it again?" another reported asked.

"I'm positive I could," I said arrogantly.

"What will you do with the money?" a reporter in the back shouted.

"I haven't decided yet," I said. "But I don't think it will be very hard to spend."

The reporters laughed. Clearly, they were impressed with me. I couldn't wait to read all their articles. I would be even more famous.

On the drive to Granger City, Grandpa had a thousand questions. I really didn't feel like explaining anything right then. Finally I claimed that I was just too tired to talk anymore. Mom had to fill him in on the rest of the story.

When we got home, there were cars parked down both sides of the street. Every light in our house was on. When I opened the door, a crowd of people yelled, "Congratulations, T. J.!"

It looked as if the whole town were there. Douglas, Shannon, Chad, and Rick were right at the front door. Coach White was there with most of the team. My teachers and some of Mom's friends stood in the background. Another reporter from the Granger City News had also showed up. He wanted to take another picture for the newspaper.

I posed for my picture in front of a big cake. The words "T. J. the *Whiz Kid*" were written in icing on top.

Then I slowly worked my way through the crowd. I answered questions about New York, the show, and the money.

The crowd slowly thinned until only a few people were left. I was hoping everyone would leave except for Rick and Chad. They were the ones I really wanted to talk to.

"I watched every show," Shannon said. "You were great."

Douglas stared at the two of us as she leaned over and kissed me on the cheek.

"Oh, thanks," I said, brushing past her to get to Chad and Rick.

"You guys stick around," I said. "I want to talk to you."

"Sure," they agreed, settling back on the couch.

"Did you say you were leaving, Douglas?" I asked.

"No," he said. "I can stick around for a while yet."

"It's getting kind of late," I said. "I don't want you to get in trouble with your parents. I'll just talk to you tomorrow."

He stared at me for a minute. Then he turned and left.

Finally I could sit and talk with Chad and Rick.

"I want you guys to go shopping with me tomorrow after school," I said. "I'm going to be looking for some new things for my room."

"Sure," Chad said.

"As you can see," I said, blushing, "our house isn't much to look at. I thought it was time I got my room updated."

"What do you want to buy?" Rick asked.

"I thought I'd start with a 25-inch TV and DVD player," I announced.

"There's a new model on the market," Chad said. "It's expensive, but it's top of the line."

"That's good because I don't want a piece of junk!" I said.

"We can recommend some good movies and music too," Rick said.

"That's great," I agreed. "And, of course, I'll also want a new computer. I want one with at least a 15-gig hard drive. I want 128 megs of RAM and a 17-inch color monitor."

"No problem," Chad said. "We'll meet you after school."

"Great!" I said.

After they left, I headed up to my room to unpack. I wanted to hang up my new clothes. It would be tough to decide what to wear on my first day back to school. After all, I had an image to keep up now.

I set my alarm for a little later the next morning. I figured the teachers wouldn't get mad at me if I was a little late.

I didn't get to enjoy those extra minutes though. Alexis came bounding into my room bright and early. She pounced on the middle of my bed, shaking me out of sleep.

"What are you doing?" I yelled angrily.

"What's your problem?" she asked.

"It's hard enough to get a good night's sleep in this old bed," I complained. "Then you wake me up before the alarm goes off!"

"You're going to be late for school," she pointed out.

"That's my problem," I said. I stared at her, waiting for her to leave.

"Okay," she muttered as she left the room.

I got dressed in my new clothes. I combed my hair until it was perfect. When I got downstairs, Douglas was waiting for me.

"What are you doing here?" I asked.

"We always ride to school together." He frowned. "What's with you?"

"Nothing," I said. "But I'm going to be late this morning. You'd better go on without me."

"Fine," he said as he slammed the front door.

"Why did Douglas slam the door when he left?" Mom asked as I entered the kitchen.

"I don't know," I said. "He's been acting weird lately."

Mom looked at me strangely. Then she asked, "Aren't you going to be late for school?"

"I wish everyone would get off my back about that!" I shrieked.

"T. J.!" she said in a warning tone. "You know better than to talk to me that way."

"Sorry," I threw out as I headed out the back door.

The only fun I had at school that day was when I could tell stories about the trip. Other than that, school was a pain. Some of the teachers actually made me work on homework that I'd missed.

As soon as school was out, I met Chad and Rick. They went with me to Appliance Barn and helped me pick out the best stuff. Because I was such a good customer, the store delivered the items right away. We had them all set up by the time Mom got home from work.

"T. J.!" she called as she came upstairs. "I was just going to—"

She stood at the door of my room and surveyed my purchases. Then she put both hands on her hips and raised one eyebrow.

"Chad and Rick," she said, "I think you both need to go home now."

"Yes, ma'am," they said. They looked grateful for the chance to escape.

Before she could say anything, I spoke up for myself.

"I got these things at a great price," I bragged. "Chad and Rick showed me the best brands to get."

She still look unconvinced, so I threw in the zinger.

"Besides, it was *my* money," I said in a tone that I shouldn't have used. "I can spend it however I want to!"

"Tanner James Westin!" she said firmly. "You will box up every one of those things and return them!"

"I don't want to return them," I said angrily.

"I can understand that you would want to buy yourself something special," she said. "But most of that money needs to be spent on important things, like your college education. I won't let you throw your money away on things you don't need."

"But I need these things," I argued. "You should see Chad's room. He has all of this and more."

"But you don't live in Chad's house," she pointed out. "You live in *our* house. And *we* cannot afford those things."

I'm not sure what happened at that point. I just know that the words I was thinking in my brain were not the same words that came out of my mouth.

"Well, I *can* afford them now," I said. "I have my own money. I'm embarrassed that I have to live in this old run-down house. I should at least be able to have some nice things in my room."

Then I saw the hurt in her eyes, and I knew I'd gone too far. Before I could apologize, she turned and left the room. I slumped down on the floor in front of my 25-inch TV. Suddenly it didn't look so great.

10

The Important Things

I spent the rest of the evening putting everything back in the boxes. Then I carefully stacked them in the corner of my room.

I could see that Mom's bedroom light was still on. I walked quietly down the hall. Softly, I knocked on her door.

"Come in," she said.

"Hey, Mom," I said, almost whispering. "I'm really sorry."

"Come here and sit down," she said gently. "I think we need to talk."

I sat down and steadied myself for a lecture.

"I didn't realize that you were embarrassed about living here," she said quietly.

"I never have been," I tried to explain. "It was just that I saw Chad's house, and he has all that great stuff. That's when I noticed how little we have."

"That reminds me," Mom said. "Why are you hanging around with Chad and Rick? What about Douglas?"

"He's around," I said. "He just bugs me sometimes."

"He's been your best friend since kindergarten," she pointed out. "He's never bugged you before."

I thought back over the last two weeks. It was true that I had blown Douglas off quite a few times. But he just didn't understand what was going on with me.

"He's changed a lot lately," I said, trying to defend my actions.

"You'd better do some thinking about who's changed a lot lately," she said.

The room was silent for a few minutes. I thought about Douglas, and the show, and how I'd been acting. I began to realize what a jerk I'd been.

"I know all that money kind of went to my head," I said slowly. "I guess I forgot why I wanted to win in the first place."

"Why *did* you want to win?" she asked.

"I only wanted to win some money to help pay the bills," I explained. "I realize that since Dad died, I'm the man of the house. It's my job to take care of us."

She stared at me for a long time. Then with tears in her eyes, she reached over to hug me.

"I've made a terrible mistake," she admitted. "I've let you to take on too many responsibilities. I've relied on you too much. You shouldn't have to take on a man's role. You're just a teenager."

"But it's something I really *want* to do," I insisted.

"You're really a fine young man, T. J.," she said. "But it's my job to be the parent, not yours. Paying the bills is my responsibility."

"I know," I said. "But I wish I could help." I paused.

"I'll think about the money some more," I continued. "And I'll talk it over with you before I spend any next time."

"That sounds like a good plan," Mom said.

As I was leaving, she stopped me again.

"I think you should consider keeping that new computer," she said softly. "Ours is kind of old. Besides, you and Alexis will really need one for school."

"Okay," I agreed.

I went back to my room and made a new list of ways to spend the money. I left it on the desk to discuss with Mom the next day. Then I nuzzled down into my old, worn bed and slept soundly.

I was waiting downstairs the next morning, but Douglas never showed up. I rode my bike to school alone. I was hoping I would be able to patch things up with him.

I didn't see him all morning. Finally I decided he was avoiding me. At lunch I went straight to the cafeteria.

Chad and Rick called for me to join them, but Douglas wasn't with them. As I made my way through the cafeteria, I saw Douglas sitting alone at our old table. I walked over to him and plopped my tray down across from him.

"Hey, Douglas!" I greeted, trying to sound normal.

"Hey," he answered quietly.

"Where were you this morning?" I asked.

"Around," he muttered. He piled his peas on his mashed potatoes.

I could see he wasn't going to budge. This was going to be tougher than I thought.

"Want to come over and watch *Whiz Kid* after school?" I invited.

"No." He frowned. "I don't ever want to hear about that show again."

"Look, Douglas," I began. "I'm really sorry about the way I've been acting lately."

"You mean acting like a big shot?" he asked angrily. "Or do you mean acting like a real jerk?"

"All that stuff is over now," I said. "I just let it go to my head."

"And you forgot that I was your best friend!" he yelled. He stuffed a big bite of peas and potatoes into his mouth.

I figured I'd better talk fast while he had his mouth full.

"I got carried away about being on TV," I explained. "But it's all over now. I'm sorry about how I acted. I just want us to be friends again."

"Oh, you do?" he shouted. "Well, isn't that special—"

He was yelling so hard that a pea came flying out and hit me right on the nose.

I saw his surprised look and started howling with laughter. He finally broke down and started laughing too. Peas and mashed potatoes squeezed out the sides of his mouth and dripped onto his shirt.

Everyone in the cafeteria stopped and stared at us, but we didn't care. It was so great to be laughing with my best friend again. I didn't care what anyone thought.

We were walking to class after lunch when Shannon appeared.

"Hi, T. J.," she said.

"Hey, Shannon."

"Do you want to come over after school today?" she asked.

I glanced at Douglas. He was bowing his head slightly, looking away.

"I'm sorry," I said, "but I can't. I have plans with Douglas today."

"Oh, okay," she said. "Maybe tomorrow."

"Yeah," I smiled, "maybe tomorrow."

✤ ✤ ✤ ✤ ✤ ✤ ✤ ✤ ✤

Douglas helped me unpack the computer again after school. We set it up together and played a few games.

When Douglas left, I went to help Mom with dinner. I told her I was ready to discuss the money.

"Okay," she said. "What have you decided?"

"First of all, I've already subtracted $2,000 for the computer and $300 for the new clothes," I started. "That leaves me with $23,400. Then I want to use $12,000 to buy you another car."

"Oh, no," she protested. "I won't let you spend your money on a car for me."

"But we can buy a used car," I pressed. "It won't cost as much, and it would still be better than our old van."

"Well, maybe . . ." she hesitated.

"We could even shop for it together," I suggested with a smile. "In three years, I'll start driving. Then I can use it and you can get a new one."

"That sounds like a smart plan," she agreed.

"I'd also like to donate $1,000 to fight Lou Gehrig's disease," I explained. "I don't really know how to do that, but I thought you might."

"Yeah, I can help you with that," Mom said, her eyes shining with tears. "We can send a check to the ALS Foundation. They'll use the money to help find a cure."

"That's what I want," I said. "I want there to be a cure for Lou Gehrig's disease."

"What about something special for yourself?" Mom asked.

"Oh, I didn't forget," I said. "I actually want to buy two things—one for me and one for Douglas."

She looked at me with a puzzled look. Once I explained, she smiled and agreed to take me shopping after dinner.

"After I buy the things for Douglas and me, I'll have about $10,000 left," I announced. "I can put that in my savings account for college."

"I'm proud of you, T. J." Mom said. "I think you've made some good choices. I'm sure Dad would agree. And I know he'd be really proud of how you've helped out around the house. Your dad was a terrific man, and you're growing up to be just like him."

Hearing her say those words meant more to me than being a seven-time winner on *Whiz Kid*.

✣ ✣ ✣ ✣ ✣ ✣ ✣ ✣ ✣

After dinner, we made the purchases I wanted for Douglas and me. It was tough to wait until the next morning to see his reaction.

He showed up right on time. I was already waiting for him.

"Douglas, I can't find my baseball glove," I lied. "Would you see if I left it in the garage?"

"Sure," he agreed.

When he opened the door to the garage, he stopped.

"Hey!" he hollered. "Look at these GT-Dyno dirt bikes! Where did they come from?"

"I bought them with the money I won," I said excitedly. "The silver one is yours. The black one is mine."

"What?" he exclaimed. "You bought *me* a bike?"

"Get on and let's go!" I yelled as I pushed him through the door. "I've been dying to try them out."

We tore down the driveway. We were up and down the block in a flash. The bikes not only looked great, they felt great too.

They even passed the ultimate test. When we got to the end of my driveway, we hit the brakes hard. The tires locked and we skidded right up to the garage door. We got off and measured our skid marks. It was a new record—7 feet, 6 inches!